the boy with the big blue HAIR

written & illustrated by

Chris Censullo

OddInt Media

OddInt

Once there was an ordinary little boy,
with the most extraordinary hair.

His hair was so thick and so lush,
that his kitty loved to lay in it.
When she did, it made him giggle.

But because his hair was bigger and bluer than any of the other children at school, sometimes they would make fun of him.

"I wish I could just look like everyone else," he sighed.

He tried hiding his hair under a hat.
Stuff, stuff, stuff. Tuck, tuck, tuck.

But it just popped right off.

He went to the barber to get it cut.
Clip, clip, clip. Snip, snip, snip.

But his hair just grew back,
bigger and bluer than ever.

He tried taming it with sticky, styling products.
Squirt, squirt, squirt, glob, glob, glob.

But that only made things worse.

"I guess big, blue hair, is part of me."

"You seem to like it, maybe I should too."
He decided, as his kitty purred from above.

The next day at school, the children pointed and laughed, as usual. "Not again," the boy groaned as he took his seat.

Suddenly, the boy began to giggle.

"Meow!" The boy's kitty popped out from amongst his big, blue hair.

Then something even more unexpected happened. A cheer arose from the class. "Hooray!" They all shouted. "There's a kitty in the classroom."

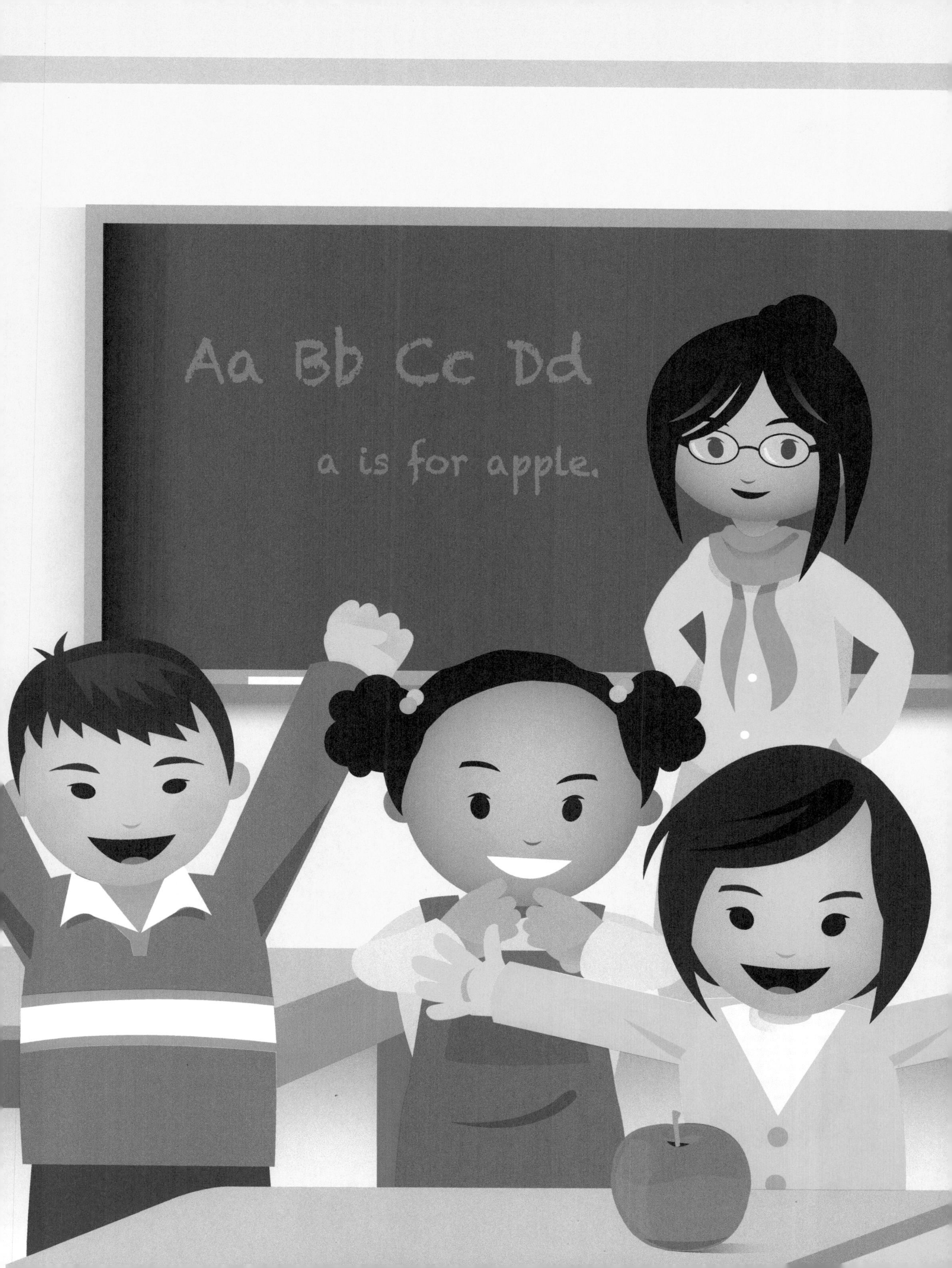
Aa Bb Cc Dd
a is for apple.

Big, blue hair, isn't so bad after all. He thought.

the end.

Thank you to my family and
friends for all their support.
This book is dedicated to my
Uncle Nick, who told me
to never stop drawing.

For more information visit cutethingsart.com
and facebook.com/TheBoyWithTheBigBlueHair

cute things

OddInt Media

OddInt

CPSIA information can be obtained at www.ICGtesting.com
Printed in the USA
LVOW01*1913200214

374579LV00001B/1/P